Dr. Hans Reinhardt: The half-crazed genius, scientist, commander of the *Cygnus* who is determined to explore the Black Hole

S.T.A.R.: Dr. Reinhardt's prototype for the sentry robots. He was the number-one robot until Reinhardt built Maximillian.

Maximillian: The monster robot who is Dr. Reinhardt's henchman

CYGNUS CREW

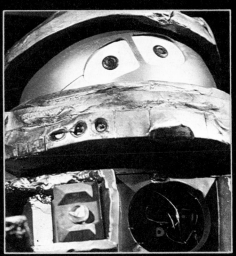

Humanoid Crew Members: Other monstrous creations of Dr. Reinhardt's; they are half-human, half-robot.

Sentry Robots: The robots assigned to guard and run the *Cygnus*

Old B.O.B.: An earlier model of V.I.N.CENT., an old-timer who eventually helps the *Palomino* crew

WALT DISNEY PRODUCTIONS presents

THE BLACK HOLE STORYBOOK

Random House New York

Story adapted by Shep Steneman
Based on the Walt Disney Productions film
Screenplay by Jeb Rosebrook and Gerry Day
Story by Jeb Rosebrook and Bob Barbash & Richard Landau
Directed by Gary Nelson

Copyright © 1979 by Walt Disney Productions. All rights reserved under International and
Pan American Copyright Conventions. Published in the United States by Random House, Inc.,
New York, and simultaneously in Canada by Random House of Canada Limited, Toronto.
Library of Congress Cataloging in Publication Data: The black hole storybook.
SUMMARY: While maintaining surveillance over a black hole, the crew of the spacecraft *Palomino*
locates a long-lost ship now manned by one human and an army of robots.   [1. Black holes
(Astronomy)—Fiction.   2. Robots—Fiction.   3. Science Fiction]   I. Disney (Walt) Productions.
PZ7.B5316   [E]   79-10623   ISBN: 0-394-84278-2 (trade)   ISBN: 0-394-94278-7 (lib. bdg.)
Manufactured in the United States of America   2 3 4 5 6 7 8 9 0

THE BLACK HOLE STORYBOOK

December 24 began much like any ordinary day aboard the U.S.S. *Palomino*. The explorer craft was homeward bound from the farthest reaches of our galaxy, but to the discouraged crew, Christmas was still a faraway dream.

Harry Booth, the mission's journalist, summed it up to his small tape recorder: "Man's long search for extra-terrestrial life in this galaxy is drawing to a close. Based upon the research of Dr. Alex Durant, this expedition has explored the last uncharted regions for eighteen months. But, like all past searches, it has found absolutely nothing."

Booth glanced at Durant. "Not exactly the way you expected to spend Christmas Eve."

The disappointed astrophysicist shrugged. "Beats fighting the mobs of last-minute shoppers."

In the command cockpit, young First Officer Charles Pizer was recalling Christmas dinners on Earth. "I'm starving!" he moaned.

"What else is new?" V.I.N.CENT. chuckled. As usual, the spunky little robot acted almost human.

"Nothing on the menu, I'm sure," Pizer replied. "What's for dinner?"

"Dehydrated turkey and dehydrated gravy. Dehyd . . ."

"Enough! Enough!" cried Pizer. "V.I.N.CENT., I envy you. You have no taste buds."

"Think we'll make it home in one piece?" Dr. Kate McCrae joked as she floated into the power complex below decks.

Captain Dan Holland gave her a fond smile. "I almost wish we weren't going home."

"Oh, there'll be other missions. I'll charm the powers that be into assigning you and V.I.N.CENT. to my team."

Holland frowned. "The 'powers that be' have other plans for our little friend. Like the scrap heap."

"I won't let them! I'll adopt him!"

"V.I.N.CENT. and I have been together a long time," Holland said, grinning. "We're a package deal."

"Well, I certainly can't adopt *you*."

"That wasn't exactly what I had in mind," Holland replied, putting his arms around the astrogeo-physicist's waist. But the mood was shattered when V.I.N.CENT.'s unromantic voice came over the intercom.

"Captain, I regret the interruption, but there is something up here I think you should see."

Holland scowled. "What's up?"

"The largest Black Hole I have ever encountered."

Holland headed for the hatch. "Hologram it. I'll be right up."

Meanwhile, in the center of the lab, the hologram's floating three-dimensional picture lit up as Kate entered the room. She saw a brilliant cloud of huge stars, fiery asteroids, and glowing gases, all swirling around a disk of utter darkness—a Black Hole.

"The most destructive force in the universe," Durant observed. "Nothing can escape it, not even light."

Kate nodded. "Some experts believe black holes will eventually devour the entire universe."

"When you see great suns sucked in and disappear without a trace, it sure makes you wonder," said Booth.

Holland entered the cockpit.

"Give us some magnification, V.I.N.CENT." The robot threw a switch, and the awesome whirlpool's image leaped closer. "It's a monster, all right," Holland muttered.

"I have picked up something else of interest," said V.I.N.CENT., polarizing the image. A huge, long man-made object was visible against the Black Hole. "It appears to be some kind of ship."

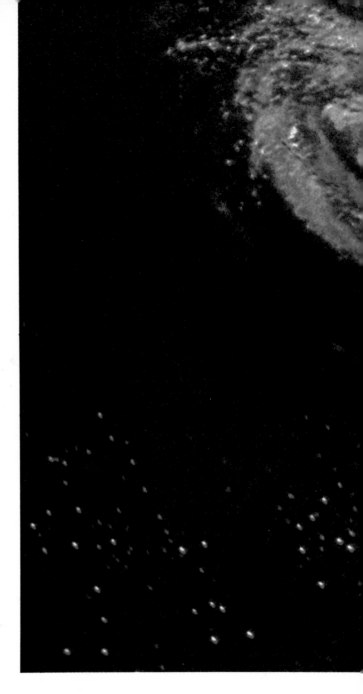

"Nobody's built one that size in years," said Holland. "Try to identify it."

Screens in both the lab and the cockpit began displaying silhouettes of spacecrafts and finally held the image of a long, ghostly shape. "That's it!" Kate gasped, turning pale.

"United States Space Probe One," said V.I.N.CENT. from the cockpit. "U.S.S. *Cygnus.* Dr. Kate, was that not the ship your father was on?"

Kate nodded weakly. "U.S.S. *Cygnus,*" she repeated in a trance. "Mission, the same as ours: to search for planetary life. Recalled to Earth twenty years ago. Mission failed."

"The 'great' Hans Reinhardt, commander," Booth snorted. "Vain. Ambitious. Refused to admit defeat. Ignored the recall."

Kate nodded grimly. "The ship just . . . vanished. They were never heard from again."

"It's a legend," Pizer said eagerly. "Get us in close, and V.I.N.CENT. and I can go aboard on tethers."

V.I.N.CENT.'s lights blinked. "Discretion, Mr. Pizer, is the better part of valor."

"It's the story of a lifetime," Booth insisted. "There's no reason to let it go untold."

"I think there is," said Holland, gazing at the Black Hole in his viewer, "and it's staring right back at us."

Kate McCrae rushed into the cockpit from the lab with a desperate look that Holland understood. "Kate, I know how you

must feel about your father. But that ship's hanging on the edge of a whirlpool."

"Yet it hasn't moved one inch since we spotted it," Durant announced from the lab. "It's defying the gravity of the Black Hole. That's definitely worth investigating."

Holland's instincts were against it, but he couldn't resist Kate's pleading eyes. "All right. We'll go in for a look." Pizer and V.I.N.CENT. turned the ship around on a course toward the *Cygnus* and then fired the thrusters. The thrusters belched flame, propelling the *Palomino* forward.

13

As the Black Hole grew nearer, a mild bump jostled the *Palomino*. "Gravitational turbulence," said Durant. "Better strap ourselves in."

The bumps grew stronger. The ship began to shake as it encountered strong jolts, each more powerful than the last. "She's bucking like a bronco!" Pizer exclaimed. "Gravity still climbing!"

"Gravity near danger zone," V.I.N.CENT. warned. "Escape threshold requires reserve power."

"We can afford one pass," Holland declared. "But we'll have to clear out in a hurry."

As the *Palomino* bucked and bounced forward, the *Cygnus* loomed larger in the viewports. Just as the big ship seemed almost close enough to touch, the jolting ceased. The ride became as smooth as glass.

Amazed, Pizer checked his gauges. "Zero gravity!"

"It's like the eye of a hurricane," said Booth. "What's happening?"

"A natural phenomenon. Or something from that ship." Durant activated the microbeam. "Look sharp."

As the *Palomino* drifted over the top of the *Cygnus*, Kate leaned closer to the viewport. The enormous superstructure below looked dark, deserted, forbidding. Not a single light was shining. There was utterly no evidence of life. "No radio contact," Pizer announced. Kate couldn't help feeling totally disheartened.

Passing over the far side of the lonely ghost ship, the *Palomino* suddenly gave a wild shudder and veered to one side. "Gravity in red

zone!" Pizer yelled to the crew.

"It's got us!" Holland shouted, fighting the controls. "We're tumbling!"

More jolts rocked the ship. Air lines above and below decks burst open and hissed like angry snakes. Booth and Durant scrambled below to make repairs while Kate worked on the damage in the lab.

As Holland and Pizer struggled to bring the ship around, V.I.N.CENT. hurried outside to secure a loose hatch. Straining against the Black Hole's intense pull, he attached himself to a tether and made his way along the ship's outer surface. But he had no radio contact with the ship. "There's no communication from V.I.N.CENT.," Pizer told Kate over the intercom. "See if you can get

through to him with your E.S.P."

Dr. McCrae shut her eyes and concentrated hard. "It works," she said. "He's coming in loud and clear. He says he's taking care of business."

Durant had grimmer news. "We can make temporary repairs on the secondary lines. But we'll have to replace parts in the main regulator, or we'll lose our oxygen supply."

Holland shook his head as he righted the *Palomino* to the proper escape angle. "Hit the boosters, Charlie!"

Outside, turning to watch the big engines fire, V.I.N.CENT. discovered something terrible. His tether had snapped in two. One arm was all that kept him from drifting into space forever, and his grip was loosening with the pull of gravity.

Kate relayed his E.S.P. call for help. "I'll go after him!" Pizer cried.

"Stay put," Holland ordered.

"What if it were one of us out there?" Pizer demanded.

"V.I.N.CENT. *is* one of us. Kate, tell him to hang on. Explain that we're trying to backtrack to that zero gravity around the *Cygnus*."

As he got the message, V.I.N.CENT. lost his grip. He felt himself being pulled toward the Black Hole. Desperately he fired a magnetic tether against the body of the *Palomino* and struggled to reel himself in. He clung to the ship with three of his arms.

Just above the *Cygnus*, the *Palomino* shuddered in the field of zero gravity. "Reverse the thrusters and look for a place to set down," Holland ordered, relaxing a little. "Kate, how's V.I.N.CENT.?"

"Still with us," she sighed.

Suddenly, incredibly, the huge dark superstructure of the ghost ship came to life. All at once the lights of the *Cygnus* began blazing brightly.

"Like a tree on Christmas morning!" Pizer marveled.

Kate brightened, too. "Someone's alive down there!" she cried, pointing to dark forms that moved within the *Cygnus*'s translucent shell. "There are people aboard!"

"Shadows of some sort, anyway," Durant replied with scientific precision.

"People, Alex," Kate insisted. "I know it. I feel it."

Captain Holland was in no mood to take chances. He ordered Pizer to lock the *Palomino*'s warheads into firing position.

"They've got to be friendly," Durant protested. "They could've blasted us out of the sky."

"The docking elevator is coming up," said Pizer. "I wonder why they didn't roll out the red carpet earlier."

"I don't know, and I don't like

it," Holland said. "But we have no choice. We've got to repair our ship."

Pizer and Holland maneuvered the *Palomino* toward the waiting dock.

Meanwhile V.I.N.CENT. landed inside the end of the connector tube as it moved toward the closed hatch of the *Palomino*. Inside Pizer and Holland picked up their laser guns. After the connector from the *Cygnus* was hooked up to the *Palomino*, Pizer checked the gravity/oxygen readout, then pushed a switch, and the airlock opened with a whoosh. V.I.N.CENT. was there to greet them. "Out of the frying pan," he said, twinkling. "Hopefully not into the fire." To the crew's delight, he was still his proverbial self.

At the far end of the connector, the door to the *Cygnus* slowly opened. No one came out to welcome them. "Charlie, you stay with the *Palomino*," Holland commanded.

Pizer looked unhappy. "But you'll need—"

Holland cut him off. "That's an order, Charlie."

"They also serve who only stand and wait, Mr. Pizer," said V.I.N.CENT.

Pizer shook his head. "Never thought I'd end up playing straight man to a tin can." He glumly returned to his post.

The rest of the crew crossed the connector and found themselves in a deserted reception area. "Hasn't been used in years," Durant said, as he looked around at the old desks, chairs, and couches of twenty years ago.

Kate shuddered. "It's eerie. I feel as though a thousand eyes are watching us. But where are they?"

The door to the connector slammed shut. Brilliant bursts of laser fire flared from the walls, disintegrating Holland's gun. V.I.N.CENT. fell backward, his arm lasers disabled. "Down, but never out," he gasped groggily as Dr. McCrae helped him up.

"So much for the friendship theory," Booth remarked.

"Not at all," replied Durant. "If they'd wanted to, they could've killed us."

Another door slid open. Beyond was a tall, wide corridor nearly half a mile long—and entirely empty. The door behind them closed and another opened instantly, revealing the entrance to a cylinder where an air car awaited them. The crew got in and were whisked to the other end of the ship where they got out and entered an elevator.

"I know I shouldn't get my hopes up," Kate said, "but it's hard not to."

Holland nodded. "Just remember one thing. The sooner we repair the *Palomino* and blast off, the better. We're too close to that Black Hole to take any chances."

The elevator opened onto a huge, round command center. Giant computers formed walls of light that silhouetted shadowy workers in long robes. A dome above looked out into space. Enormous monitors screened views of the Black Hole. A mammoth control console dominated the center of the room.

"Stupendous!" Durant murmured, awestruck.

"Ought to be," grumped Booth. "Cost the taxpayers enough."

Kate stepped toward the computers. "This is Kate McCrae," she said. "Is Officer Frank McCrae aboard?" The workers didn't respond.

Sensing danger, V.I.N.CENT. flashed his warning lights. From the control console, a huge metallic red shape glided toward them. A pulse of red light glowed in the giant's head like the eye of a Cyclops.

Holland grabbed his communicator. "Charlie, do you read me?" There was no response.

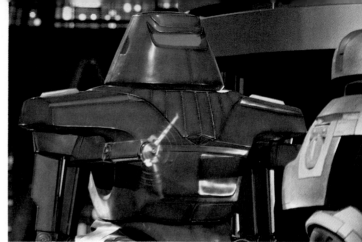

Advancing on the group, the hulking robot thrust forth long metallic arms with sharp, whirling hooks at the ends. V.I.N.CENT. instantly jumped out to defend his friends. The red monster floated up to him and stopped.

"A ship of robots and computers," Booth growled.

"With this . . . thing in charge," Durant muttered.

"Not quite, Dr. Durant." A deep voice startled them from behind. "This is Maximillian. He and my other robots only run the ship the way I wish it run."

"How do you know my name?" Durant demanded.

"You have been monitored ever since our sensors first detected you. Welcome aboard the ship *Cygnus*."

Booth squinted into the darkness. "Dr. Hans Reinhardt! You always did have a flair for theatrical entrances."

"Your flair, Mr. Booth, was for a poison pen." His aging face intense and powerful, Reinhardt stepped into the light and cast a hateful look at Booth. Then, softening his manner, he turned toward Kate. "My dear child, I'm sorry to dash your hopes. Your father is dead. He was a man to be proud of."

Kate trembled, and Holland put a reassuring hand on her shoulder. "What about the rest of the crew?" he asked.

Reinhardt seemed surprised. "They didn't return?"

Holland shook his head grimly.

"Terrible," said Dr. Reinhardt. "They were a fine crew. A field of meteorites disabled us, and we were adrift without communications. Officer McCrae and I chose to remain aboard, but I ordered the others to abandon ship and head home. We never knew what happened to them."

The elevator opened behind him, and metallic man-sized sentry robots shoved Pizer out. "They came to get me," Pizer said to Holland. "Quite a goon squad!"

Reinhardt dismissed the sentries and addressed the group. "You were disarmed for your safety. My robots are programed to respond to any act of aggression. But rest assured, you're not prisoners. You're my guests."

"I hope somebody told the robots that," Pizer muttered under his breath.

"Doctor, if you were monitoring us, you must have picked up our signals," said Holland.

Reinhardt nodded.

"But you failed to reply."

"A slight communication problem. But now you must concentrate on your ship. Maximillian, take them to Maintenance. Give them whatever they need for repairs."

As the red hulk moved toward Pizer and Holland, he shoved V.I.N.CENT. aside. The little robot jumped in front of him and blocked his way.

"Back off, V.I.N.CENT.," said Pizer.

"Not until he does," V.I.N.CENT. replied firmly. Maximillian's red light grew hotter.

The commander of the *Cygnus* was amused. "A classic confrontation—David and Goliath. But this time David's overmatched. That's enough, Maximillian. Remember, these are our guests." The huge robot backed away.

"All communication problems aside," Holland whispered to Kate as he left, "Reinhardt waited a long time to show any lights."

Deep inside the *Cygnus*, Maximillian led Pizer and Holland to a dimly lit stockroom with rows and rows of shelves. Behind the control desk slept a weary old robot—a battered, twenty-year-old model much like V.I.N.CENT. Maximillian swatted him to the floor. The old robot lit up and backed away.

V.I.N.CENT. introduced himself. "V.I.N.CENT.: Vital Information Necessary Centralized. Labor Force Three Ninety-Sixth." The other robot deliberately ignored him.

V.I.N.CENT. tried again. "I see by your markings you're from the old two-eight." The battered old robot continued to ignore him and moved off down a row of shelves.

Holland headed for the door. "Charlie, I'll go up to the *Palomino* and start taking that regulator apart." Maximillian started after him.

Pizer moved to distract Maximillian. "Dr. Reinhardt told you to order parts for us, Max," Pizer said firmly. He confused Maximillian long enough for Holland to step through the door.

"Well, get cracking!" Pizer ordered. "We need E.C.S. valves, demand pressure regulators, and . . ." Glowering, Maximillian plugged himself into a computer. Drawers began opening around the room.

Reinhardt led the others on a tour of the ship. "You repaired the damage to the *Cygnus*," Booth reminded him. "Why didn't you obey the order to return to Earth?"

"There were other worlds yet to be explored, Mr. Booth. Life dreams unrealized."

"Your refusal would still be considered piracy."

Reinhardt seemed annoyed. "To become what we are capable of becoming, Mr. Booth, is the only end in life. I am about to prove it." He pointed to a viewport. Below, connected to the main body of the *Cygnus* by a catwalk, eight neutron reactors glowed with power. "There's enough energy here to supply all the Earth."

Durant beamed with enthusiasm. "Do you mean to turn this technology over to us?"

"This is just the beginning," Reinhardt boasted. "It's high time others learned of their mistakes and my successes. Come along, and I'll explain about our power

source. We use a new element. I have named it Cygnium."

Preoccupied with the sound of his own voice, Reinhardt didn't notice Booth slip into the shadows and set off in the opposite direction. Opening a door, the journalist stumbled into a bright, warm room where a forest of fruits and vegetables grew in hydroponic tanks—vats filled with water and nutrients.

A robot was at the control panel. Beneath its flowing robe, the robot seemed to have a human shape, but its face was just an expressionless mirror. Rising from its seat, the robot limped out the door.

Suddenly something clicked in the journalist's mind. Limping? A robot? Booth wondered, but when he popped out of the door for another look, the corridor was empty.

Holland had been investigating, too. He had found a room that had obviously been the crew's quarters. Most of the contents hadn't been touched in years. Musty old footlockers gathered dust. Faded pinups and yellowed, outdated calendars hung from the walls. Yet the bunks themselves were rumpled, as though they were still in use.

Holland opened a door that led to a vaulted, cathedral-like chamber. As he watched from the shadows, six robed robots lifted a covered form into a cylinder in the outside wall. In unison, and with great solemnity, the robots stepped back. The shrouded form sped through the cylinder out into space, and floated gently to the edge of the *Cygnus's* zero-gravity

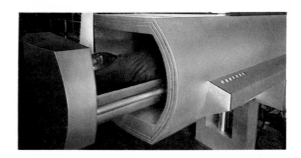

field. Then the Black Hole's force sucked the form away like a missile.

Holland was puzzled, but he didn't have much time for thought. Maximillian suddenly appeared, his red eye smoldering. "Must've made a wrong turn," Holland apologized weakly. Maximillian watched him as he backtracked through the crew's quarters and turned toward the *Palomino*.

Reinhardt laughed as he and the *Palomino*'s scientists returned to the *Cygnus* command center. "Aha! So black holes do interest you."

"They fascinate me," Durant replied. "And the way you've defied the power of this one with your anti-gravity force overwhelms me, sir. Your discoveries must have helped compensate for the loneliness out here."

"Loneliness? Not when a man has the entire universe to keep him company. It has been said that only alone can a man achieve

his full potential for greatness. Dr. Durant, I suspect you are a man who longs for greatness—but has not yet found his true direction."

"Perhaps I'll find it here," said Durant. "That is, if you're in no rush for us to leave."

Kate frowned. Dr. Reinhardt's influence over Dr. Durant was growing every minute. She did not like it at all.

When he returned to the *Cygnus* after a long day of repair work aboard the *Palomino*, V.I.N.CENT. found that Reinhardt had issued an invitation to his human cohorts.

"We're only having dinner," Holland assured him.

"The spider said that to the fly," V.I.N.CENT. noted. "I should be with you."

Pizer pointed through the door to the robot recreation center. "Hey! You'll have the time of your life in there," Pizer said.

"I don't mean to sound superior," V.I.N.CENT. replied, "but I hate the company of robots."

"Remember what they say about all work and no play," Pizer chided.

V.I.N.CENT. walked into the shooting gallery. A line of sentry robots was standing at attention,

waiting to be called to the firing line. At the end of the line was the old robot V.I.N.CENT. had met in the stockroom.

At that moment two robots were firing their last rounds, and the one on the right, who was shiny black, was the winner by a large margin.

V.I.N.CENT. walked over to the old robot.

"Who's the flashy black hat?"

"That's S.T.A.R.," replied the old robot. "He was number one until Reinhardt built Maximillian."

"Did you ever go up against him?"

"Only once," said the old robot. "And I beat him. It upset him so much he blew a fuse."

To the crew of the *Palomino*, the crystal chandeliers, wood-paneled

walls, comfortable old chairs, and plush carpet of the *Cygnus* dining room were a welcome change from their usual metal-and-plastic surroundings. The food was even more welcome—a feast of fruits, vegetables, and hot dishes, all

wondrously fresh. Only the face-less humanoid robots serving the meal spoiled the effect.

"We begin with fresh mushroom soup prepared from my own personal garden," Reinhardt proclaimed.

"I remember writing about your agricultural station," said Booth. "Large enough to support the entire crew, wasn't it?"

Reinhardt nodded. "These days, it's tiny. Only enough for one."

Before Booth could disagree,

Maximillian barged in with a message. Reinhardt read it, beamed, and dismissed him. Then he raised his glass. "Tonight, my friends, we stand on the brink of a feat unparalleled in space exploration. If the data on my returning probe ship match my expectations, I will travel where no man has dared to go. The *Cygnus* will take me in . . . through . . . and beyond the Black Hole!"

The idea astounded everyone. Except Harry Booth. "Totally im-

possible!" he muttered.

Reinhardt flushed with anger. "'Impossible' is a word found only in the dictionary of fools!"

"People have dreamed your dream for years, Doctor," said Pizer. "How do you expect the *Cygnus* to escape being crushed by the forces in there?"

"My anti-gravity force field can withstand that stress. And the course I've chosen will take us in at an angle that will shoot us through. If I stay on course, even the heat will not affect us. My probes have confirmed it."

"Fantastic!" marveled Durant. "Then you must want the *Palomino* to stand by and monitor your journey."

Reinhardt nodded. "To a new world—another place and time. I assure you, I will be victorious."

Kate was unconvinced. "What role will people play in this new world of yours?"

"Perhaps none. On board this ship I have the beginning of an entirely self-sustaining mechanical civilization. It responds to my orders and . . ."

Maximillian lumbered in, his light blinking evenly. "Excuse me," said Reinhardt, gesturing toward the viewport. "My probe ship will be docking momentarily. Please continue your meal." He followed Maximillian out the door.

"That man is walking a tightrope between genius and insanity!" Kate proclaimed.

"He's an out-and-out liar, anyhow," said Booth. "That 'tiny' one-man garden of his is big enough to feed an army."

"Nothing strange about that,"

Durant responded, rushing to Dr. Reinhardt's defense. "It purifies the air."

"Tell 'em about the funeral, Dan," Pizer urged. "A robot funeral. Almost human."

"The robot gardener was almost human, too. Even had a limp," Booth reported.

"A malfunction, Harry," Durant surmised.

Booth shook his head. "I'm telling you I was looking at some kind of . . . person."

Durant grew impatient. "What are you suggesting?"

"That we get off this ship and head home as soon as possible," said Holland.

"Why not take the *Cygnus* and Reinhardt home with us?" Booth suggested. "We've got two scientists to reprogram the computers and robots, three of us to take care of Reinhardt and his monster. We'd be heroes."

"We could also be dead," Holland said grimly. "My job is to get you all off this ship alive."

After striking up a friendship with his distant relative in the shooting gallery, V.I.N.CENT. sneaked out and met him in the stockroom. "My name's B.O.B.," said the old robot. "I'm the last of

us here. I couldn't talk freely until now. If Maximillian knew, it would mean the end for both of us."

V.I.N.CENT. blinked agreement. "Do you have lasers in here?"

"We should have a few," B.O.B. said, searching. "V.I.N.CENT., there's something you should know about this ship. Your friends could be in grave danger—follow me, please."

V.I.N.CENT. followed Old B.O.B. down a long corridor and through a double door. Before them, lying on revolving operating tables, humanoid robots received beams of colored laser light from above. Humanoid robot surgeons worked the computer controls.

"These poor creatures are what's left of the crew," B.O.B. explained. "They're kept alive electronically."

V.I.N.CENT. could hardly believe his eyes. "Humans?"

"More robot than human now. Their brains have been altered to do Reinhardt's bidding. They react only to their assigned duties. They're—"

Two sentry robots burst through the door behind them. "Get down!" V.I.N.CENT. ordered. As the sentries raised their weapons, V.I.N.CENT. blasted them off their feet with his arm lasers. Aware of nothing but their duties, the humanoids never noticed.

V.I.N.CENT. handed B.O.B. the fallen sentries' laser guns. "How long before they'll start searching for these two?"

"Not long."

"Then we'll have to hurry back to the *Palomino* and alert Captain Holland. I'll lead the way," said V.I.N.CENT.

Durant paced the dining room. "So Reinhardt neglected his duty to his country for a higher duty. He's willing and eager to share his knowledge with us. I won't allow you to rush us away, Dan."

Holland stood firm. "I won't give you any more time, Alex."

"Well, that's really up to Dr. Reinhardt, isn't it?"

"Dan," Kate interrupted, concentrating urgently on her E.S.P., "V.I.N.CENT. wants you to meet him right away. Aboard the *Palomino*."

Holland and Pizer leaped into motion, and Booth jogged along behind them. They hurried through the main corridor, into the elevator, and then took the air car back to the reception area.

When they finally reached the *Palomino*, B.O.B. had a dismal story to tell. "When Dr. Reinhardt ignored the orders to return home, the crew turned to Officer McCrae and tried to take control of the ship. Reinhardt called it mutiny. He killed Officer McCrae and turned his sentry robots on the others. The rebellion soon ended." Then B.O.B. explained about the humanoid robots.

"We can't just leave those poor devils behind," Holland said determinedly.

"You must," Old B.O.B. replied. "The damage is irreversible. Death is their only release."

V.I.N.CENT. interrupted. "Captain, I was forced to destroy two sentry robots. The others are searching now. If they are found—"

Holland cut him off and turned to Pizer. "Charlie, start the countdown. V.I.N.CENT., tell Kate I want her and Alex back here on the double."

In the *Cygnus* command tower, Reinhardt ordered the humanoids to prepare the reactors. "We are almost ready to embark on our voyage to a new beginning," he said as the ship began to throb with power. "To a universe suspended in time, where so-called laws of nature simply do not apply. To a universe of life forever."

Durant was convinced. "I know you've achieved all this on your own, Doctor. You have every right to refuse me, but . . ."

"You wish to join me?"

Durant nodded.

"Dan wants us back on board," Kate announced, concentrating on her E.S.P. "They're ready to blast off."

"I'm staying," Durant insisted. "There's a whole new world out there. We'll be the first to explore it."

Kate took him aside. "Alex, don't throw your life away. You'll—" Another E.S.P. message interrupted her. She turned grim.

"We've got to get back, Alex," Kate insisted. "Reinhardt's a murderer. Worse. Those creatures over there were humans once—the original crew."

Dr. Reinhardt joined them. "You look ill, Dr. McCrae."

Staring at the robots in disbelief, Durant stalled for time. "She's upset at my decision to remain aboard."

Reinhardt smiled. "She's also electing to accompany us."

"No!" Kate cried.

"Your E.S.P. will ensure that news of our success gets back to the *Palomino* and the world. You will be helping to complete the mission your father gave his life for."

Durant ran up to a humanoid and tore open its reflective mask. A lifeless, emotionless, zombielike face stared back. The scientist drew away in horror.

"You might as well let me go," said Kate. "I won't send any messages."

"Maximillian!" Reinhardt commanded. "See that Dr. McCrae receives medical treatment at once."

"Let her go!" Durant shouted, hurrying toward Kate. Maximillian whirled and cut him down with a burst of laser fire.

"If there's any justice at all, Reinhardt," Kate said icily as the sentries led her away, "that Black Hole will be your grave."

Reinhardt's voice boomed out over the *Palomino*'s communicator. "You are cleared for lift-off. Dr. Durant and Dr. McCrae have chosen to stay aboard."

V.I.N.CENT. lit up with an incoming E.S.P. message. "False. Maximillian killed Dr. Durant. Dr. Kate's being taken to that so-called hospital."

Holland grabbed his laser gun. "Get Old B.O.B. to show us the fastest way there. Charlie, you stay behind. Get the ship off before the gravity pull's too strong, no matter what."

"You'll need help aboard the *Cygnus*," Pizer protested.

"That's an order," Holland snapped. He and the robots moved out.

"Fire the thrusters!" Reinhardt commanded. The giant rockets of the *Cygnus* blazed with light, and the ship slowly strained into motion.

Suddenly an alarm bell sounded. On a television screen two sentry robots in the hospital displayed their fallen counterpart. "Our troops must now liquidate our guests—except for the robot and the girl," Reinhardt told Maximillian. "And do not damage their ship."

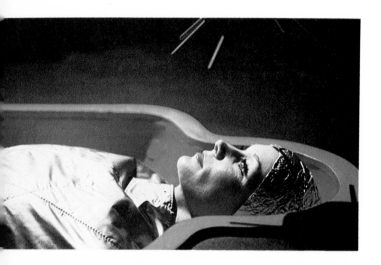

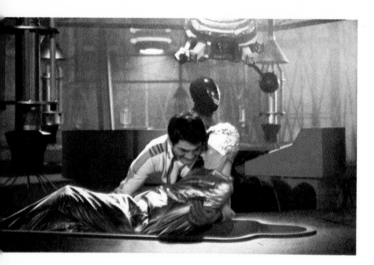

Colored laser beams illuminated the area above Kate's head as two sentry robots strapped her to the revolving operating table in the hospital. Slowly the table rotated toward the surgical laser lights. Straining her E.S.P. to the limit, she sent one last plea for help.

At that moment one of the lights was shot out. Lasers at the ready, Holland and V.I.N.CENT. had stormed through the door, with B.O.B. right behind.

One of the sentry robots reached for a red button. V.I.N.CENT. blasted him onto the operating table, and the lasers destroyed him in a sputter of sparks. In the meantime, Kate was still moving closer to the deadly beams, so Holland quickly fired at the turntable mechanism. It screeched to a halt. For now, Kate was safe.

On their TV screen, Reinhardt and Maximillian saw two humanoids start down the corridor from the hospital. The humanoids were really Holland and Kate in disguise. Rushing the other way, three sentries tried to enter the operating room, but Holland whirled and blasted them. B.O.B. and V.I.N.CENT. hurried out from behind the doors and caught up with their disguised friends.

"Have the sentries fire on all humanoids between medical and the *Palomino*!" Dr. Reinhardt commanded Maximillian.

Holland, Kate, and their robot companions ducked around a corner just in time to avoid fire from the corridor. "They're onto us," said Holland, ripping off his mask. "Maybe we can catch them in crossfire. V.I.N.CENT., you and B.O.B. try to get behind them."

V.I.N.CENT. and B.O.B. sped up the corridor side by side, then split up and dived toward the sentries. The advancing robots didn't know which way to turn. B.O.B. swooped low between two of them. Missing him, they blasted each other.

As Kate and Holland hurried down a catwalk, V.I.N.CENT. looped in the air and dive-bombed two sentries who had him in their sights. Then a wounded robot winged B.O.B. "V.I.N.CENT.!" Kate shouted as she turned and zapped B.O.B.'s attacker. "B.O.B.'s hurt!"

V.I.N.CENT. zipped over and helped the old robot up. "Are you all right?"

"First fighting I've done in years," B.O.B. said proudly. "I wish it had been Reinhardt and Maximillian themselves."

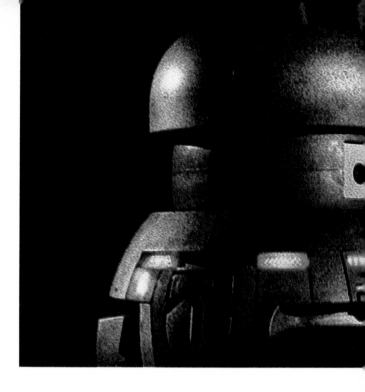

Holland's voice on the communicator broke the tense silence in the *Palomino*. "Time's up, Charlie. Take her away."

Pizer shook his head. "Where are you?"

"Blast off, Mr. Pizer!" The communicator went dead.

Pizer jumped to his feet and headed toward the door. Booth blocked his way. "You heard the captain!"

"You're pretty big on talking heroics," Pizer retorted. "Now let's see some."

Pizer charged across the connector with Booth right behind. A sentry robot fired at them. As the robot exploded under Pizer's blast, Booth grabbed his shin and fell to the floor. "I'm hit!" he groaned. "My leg!"

"Then get back to the ship!" Pizer told him. "Make sure they don't get aboard!"

Pizer crept around a corner to investigate some very suspicious noises. From behind a barricade, a line of robot sentries aimed heavy fire at his crewmates. From where Pizer stood, the robots were sitting ducks. With a wild whoop, he sent a long blast of laser fire at them. Then Kate, Holland, V.I.N.CENT., and B.O.B. stormed the barricade. They all rushed toward the *Palomino*.

If Booth was hurt, he certainly didn't show it. Scurrying into the explorer craft like a scared rabbit, he plunked himself down in the captain's chair. He was no pilot, but he had learned something about running the ship. In a frenzy, he programed computers and threw switches. The *Palomino* rumbled as the thrusters fired up.

The others reached the connector just as it slid away. They
were too late. The *Palomino* was
lifting off.

"If I'd done what Reinhardt wanted," Kate said bitterly, "you'd all be aboard."

Holland shook his head. "I'd still have gone after you."

"Look!" cried Pizer at the viewport. The *Palomino* had begun to wobble. Then it veered crazily toward the *Cygnus.*

"That ship's out of control!" cried Reinhardt in the command tower. "Blow it up before it hits us! Fire!" Maximillian aimed the *Cygnus's* space cannons and shot laser beams at the falling *Palomino.* The explorer craft blew up with a blinding flash. Breaking free, one of its thrusters crashed

down upon the *Cygnus*'s power center. The reactors exploded in a great cloud of gas.

V.I.N.CENT. and B.O.B. hovered to keep their balance as the *Cygnus* rocked, and the others grabbed the walls of the reception area. They began to think they might be doomed.

"What now?" Kate moaned.

V.I.N.CENT. blinked. "Where there's a will—"

"Reinhardt's probe ship!" Holland exclaimed. "V.I.N.CENT., you're a genius! B.O.B., what's the quickest way?"

"The air car," said B.O.B. "I'll lead the way."

At the starry outer fringes of the Black Hole, tiny asteroids began pelting the *Cygnus*'s outer surface. Larger ones soon followed. Then a real giant crashed across the bow. In an instant, the entire reception area was destroyed. Fortunately the *Palomino*'s survivors had made it to the air car just in time. From the jolted air-car cylinder, they saw space aglow.

Under the growing gravity force, the cylinder buckled and twisted, sending the air car back and forth madly. Another car approached on a head-on collision course. The sentries in the other car fired their lasers, but the car's jouncing deflected their aim. As the cylinder broke open, Holland swerved his car. Still firing, the sentries burst through their end of the cylinder and went hurtling into space.

The *Palomino* crew jumped off. B.O.B. led them across a catwalk. Crashing through the ceiling, a fiery asteroid began rolling toward them. They dived for cover just an instant before it completely demolished the catwalk. Just as they were breathing sighs of relief, there was more laser fire.

Chased by other sentries, they rushed into the agricultural station. A barrage of asteroids ripped open the dome above. The module was gripped by decompression. Bursting apart, the hydroponic tanks glazed the floor with ice. In the howling winds, frozen vegetables became deadly missiles.

"Hang on to me," B.O.B. told Kate. She grabbed his arms.

Convinced he could outrun the dogged sentries, V.I.N.CENT. zigzagged across the ice. Suddenly the sky dome ripped wider and flying vegetables began to whirl up toward it. Old B.O.B.'s controls began to freeze up. Just when the cyclone was about to carry him away, Holland dragged him to the floor. Behind them, their metallic pursuers stiffened and spiraled up through the hole in the dome.

Kate's teeth chattered and her whole body shook as V.I.N.CENT. freed the frozen door to the corridor with his lasers. Pizer and Holland dragged the immobile B.O.B. to safety and locked the door behind them. They stamped their feet and rubbed their hands to get warm.

Kate and Holland put their arms around B.O.B. to thaw him out, moving the stricken robot along between them. B.O.B.'s lights began to flicker faintly. Suddenly the sky dome in the agricultural module gave way behind them, its explosive force buckling their corridor. Everyone hung on.

With awesome force, a mammoth asteroid crashed into the command tower's superstructure. Reinhardt and Maximillian fell backward against the control board. Humanoid robots tumbled from their posts at the computers. Equipment swayed back and forth. The huge astro-screen dangled ominously.

Reinhardt struggled to his feet. "Red alert!" he announced. "We may need the probe ship! Program it!"

The asteroid shower ended as quickly as it had begun, but the *Palomino*'s survivors began to wonder if they'd ever reach the probe ship. Before them, the damaged catwalk across the power center swayed precariously. "Any way around this?" Holland asked B.O.B.

"No, Captain. And we can't go back."

"Okay. Take Kate across."

Frightened, she grasped B.O.B.'s arms tightly, and he slowly carried her away. V.I.N.CENT. and Pizer went next. To gain precious time, Holland decided to make it across on his own, but as he stepped onto the wobbly catwalk, it snapped in the middle. Holland rode the structure down until it slammed

him against a wall. Bleeding, in pain, he tried to climb back up, but he hadn't the strength. Gas from the leaking reactors began to choke him.

Suddenly V.I.N.CENT. and Old B.O.B. appeared through the thickening clouds. They grabbed Holland between them and lifted him to safety.

In the command tower, Reinhardt was triumphant. The *Cygnus* had survived the asteroid shower, and he was confident it would hold up in the Black Hole. "Power to maximum," he ordered. "We're going through."

Maximillian threw a switch. The whole ship shook in the growing gravity field. But the damaged power center could not take the strain. One of the reactors collapsed, and it exploded into space.

The entire ship was plunged into darkness. Maximillian threw the auxiliary energy banks into action, but the lights just flickered dimly. The *Cygnus* was adrift, powerless against the Black Hole's deadly grip.

Weakened parts of the ship began to break away. The command tower swayed back and forth. Reinhardt ordered Maximillian to prepare the probe ship.

Suddenly the huge astro-screen crashed down from above, pinning Reinhardt underneath. He struggled to free himself, but the screen was too heavy. "Maximillian!" he cried. "Help me!" But the robot was descending in the elevator and could not hear.

"You there! Help me!" Reinhardt shouted, but the humanoid robots did not respond. They stuck to their programed chores. "Fools! Listen to me!" Reinhardt pleaded. No one answered him. He was all alone with the zombies he had created.

Holland and his companions

reached the catwalk near the probe ship. "Look out!" Kate cried.

Maximillian loomed up behind them. B.O.B. jumped toward him, but the red hulk blasted the old robot with laser fire. V.I.N.CENT. shot back with perfect aim; Maximillian's lasers were destroyed.

"Get to the ship," V.I.N.CENT. told the others. "I'll handle this." He aimed his lasers at Maximillian's midsection, but the fire bounced away harmlessly.

As the humans ran through the ship's wreckage, Maximillian extended his whirling hooks and turned all his red rage on V.I.N.CENT. One hook caught V.I.N.CENT. hard, tumbling him against the wall. Quickly he ducked through a hole and got a firm grip on some wreckage outside.

Maximillian forced his way out and closed in for the final blow. Suddenly a cutting tool sprang out from V.I.N.CENT.'s body and thrust upward through his adversary's plating. The red behemoth's circuitry shorted. Sparks sputtered from his chest. Jerking crazily and bursting into flame, Maximillian spun off toward the Black Hole.

V.I.N.CENT. made his way inside. "You did well," B.O.B. told him feebly.

"Thanks to you, friend. I'll get you aboard now."

"No," said B.O.B., his lights growing faint. "Carry on. Help your friends. . . ." B.O.B.'s lights went out forever.

V.I.N.CENT. sadly dimmed his own panels, but only for a moment. He knew his friends would need all the help he could give them.

As the crew crossed the sharply twisted wreckage of the *Cygnus* toward the leaning probe ship, the

gravity current made every inch a struggle. Crossing some wreckage, Kate tripped and nearly swung away toward the Black Hole, but Holland pulled her in. Grabbing for Holland's arm, Pizer lost his grip and flew backward. Luckily, V.I.N.CENT. was there to catch him.

Once aboard the tiny probe, Holland and Pizer strapped themselves in at the controls. Through the viewport, Kate saw the *Cygnus* command tower wobbling wildly. Suddenly it toppled and ripped away from the rest of the ship. The whole tower, with Reinhardt, his humanoids, and his grandiose schemes, went tumbling toward the Black Hole.

"We'd better get off!" cried Pizer. "The whole ship's breaking up!"

Holland threw a final lever, and the probe lifted away. Below, the *Cygnus* buckled and bent, snapping into smaller and smaller fragments, space junk drawn irretrievably toward the Black Hole.

Flipping switches, Holland tried to set a course away from the Black Hole, but none of the controls would respond. Holland tried other panels. Nothing worked. "I can't turn her around!" he cried.

V.I.N.CENT. plugged himself into the console. "This ship has been programed," he reported.

Holland nodded. "To Reinhardt's course."

Pizer was astonished. "You mean we're going into the Black Hole?"

"Check." Holland exhaled resignedly.

"Let's pray Reinhardt was a genius," Kate said softly.

"He who hesitates is lost!" V.I.N.CENT. babbled frantically. "A rolling stone gathers no moss!" Pizer patted him on the back to calm him down.

The ship began to spin. They were in the whirlpool for real, experiencing speed, gravity, turbulence, light flashes, color waves, heat, pressure, and fear. Then they slept. It was a calm, dark, empty sleep, finally brought to an end by a dazzling white light.

The crew opened their eyes. Speechless, they watched the blinding brilliance grow dimmer. In a mysterious universe no one was certain he had ever seen before, the spacecraft was headed toward a distant star, the brightest in the sky. The survivors of the U.S.S. *Palomino* put the Black Hole behind them forever.

Captain Dan Holland: The veteran commander of the explorer craft *Palomino*

First Officer Charles Pizer: Captain Holland's young assistant

Dr. Kate McCrae: An astro-geophysicist who works with Dr. Durant

PALOMINO CREW

Dr. Alex Durant: A scientist assigned to the mission to search for life on other planets

V.I.N.CENT.: A squat, cocky little robot who looks after the *Palomino* crew

Harry Booth: A journalist, assigned to cover the expedition